Face-to-Face
with
The Duck

Text by Pascale Hédelin

Photos by the Colibri Agency

ini Charlesbridge

 *A male mallard duck (inset) rests on a log.*

Reeds offer a safe place for ducks to hide.

In the marsh

It is autumn. The pond is calm after the rain. Only a few sounds break the silence. A mallard stands near the pond, sheltered by reeds. Soon it will migrate south for the winter.

Mallards live in ponds and marshes, both in the wild and in cities. They can be found throughout the Northern Hemisphere.

3

Perfect equipment

Ducks are at home both in the water and in the air. Thanks to their webbed feet, ducks are strong swimmers. Their waterproof feathers keep them dry and warm. Ducks preen their feathers by running their bill along each one. This helps ducks waterproof their wings and straighten ruffled feathers. Ducks also have air sacs under their belly that act like buoys so they can float on the water.

 Male mallards, called drakes, have a green head with a white stripe around their neck.

Ducks have three toes on each webbed foot.

Ducks use their bill to spread their body oil across their feathers, making them waterproof.

Female mallards, called hens, are brown with an orange and black bill.

5

A mallard can spread its wings and fly straight up from the water.

Both the male and the female mallard have a blue and white patch on their wings.

Fly, duck, fly!

Ducks usually travel in pairs, in flocks, or with their young. Every day ducks fly from pond to pond in search of more food.

To take off, a duck jumps out of the water, pushing down with its feet. Ducks are heavy, so they have to keep flapping their wings to stay in the air. They can fly very well, though, and can travel long distances.

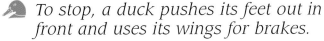 *To stop, a duck pushes its feet out in front and uses its wings for brakes.*

Time to eat

Ducks eat seeds, water plants, insects, and small fish. Some ducks, such as mallards, are called "dabbling ducks." They feed by dunking just their head underwater, leaving their tail up in the air. Their long, spoon-shaped bill is perfect for digging in the mud. "Diving ducks," such as ring-necked ducks, live in larger bodies of water and dive completely underwater to find food.

Dabbling ducks feed in shallow, muddy waters, which are full of food.

Mallards filter water through their bill, which is equipped with little plates that hold in the food.

Mallards do not dive completely underwater.

In the autumn, mallards will eat seeds on the ground.

q

 Ducks must beware of predators such as foxes, coyotes, and hawks.

  *Mallards get along well with other waterfowl, such as geese.*

In a flock, ducks are so plentiful that their enemies do not know which one to choose.

All for one

As ducks move about in search of food, they must also be on the lookout for predators. One duck alerts the others to danger by crying out. Once alerted, the flock flies away together, confusing the predator.

But predators do not attack just the ducks. Some predators, such as skunks, also prey on duck eggs.

Males cry out in a hoarse voice. Only females say, "Quack, quack."

Mating

At last winter arrives, and ducks begin to gather in giant flocks to court a mate.

To charm the female, the male preens himself and makes funny gestures. He spreads his wings and jumps about in a courtship dance.

A female signals she is ready to mate.

A mallard pair will stay together all winter.

He pushes his bill around in the water, fluffs himself up, spits out water, whistles, and pretends to groom himself. The female chooses a male and then signals to him that she is ready to mate. The male usually stays with the female until she is ready to nest.

In a flock, when one male starts a courtship dance, others will soon follow.

A female duck keeps her eggs warm for about 30 days, then they hatch.

 *If a magpie threatens her nest, the female duck will distract the bird.*

A downy nest

Soon spring arrives. Far from the pond, the female duck finds a well-protected hollow between some rocks to build her nest. She makes a nest of down, which she has pulled from her own breast, and grass. She lays from seven to 15 eggs. Camouflaged in her brown feathers, she watches over her eggs alone.

When she leaves the nest, the duck hides her eggs under some feathers to keep them warm.

A big family

After a month the little ones use their beaks to break out of their shells. When they hatch, the ducklings are moist, but their down soon dries.

 The family heads toward the pond soon after the ducklings hatch.

16

To protect the ducklings from enemies, their mother keeps them close together.

After hatching, a duckling can swim and catch small prey, but it cannot fly yet.

A mother keeps her babies warm and protected for 2 months.

The family leaves the nest and goes to the pond. Lively and clever, the ducklings already know how to swim and feed themselves. Still, they do not leave their mother's side.

new clothes

By summer the little ones are now fledglings. Fledglings are old enough to leave the nest, but lack the feathers they need to fly.

For the adult ducks, it is now time for their plumage to change.

Fledglings cannot fly.

When molting, males lose their bright feathers.

Once the fledglings have left the nest, their mother molts.

Their old feathers fall out, or molt. New ones grow in their place. Once a duck starts to molt, it cannot fly. To protect itself, it hides in the vegetation for a month. Male ducks turn brown during the molting season. In autumn they will get a new coat of colored feathers.

newcomers

Autumn ends, and the white coat of winter covers everything in snow. In harsher climates there is not as much food during winter. Ducks from these colder places fly away and spend the winter where the weather is nicer and there is more food. Most ducks migrate, but those that come from warmer areas have less distance to fly to be comfortable in the winter.

 Ducks use the sun and stars as their guide during migration.

Migrating ducks mix with those that do not leave their region during the winter.

🦆 *Ducks can stand the cold thanks to their thick down and a layer of fat.*

Beware of humans!

Most ducks are used to humans —in cities they do not fear them. But in the wild, ducks are wary of hunters. Hunters know the ducks' habits. They watch when ducks move between their resting and feeding places and notice their migration patterns. Each year in the United States, hunters kill millions of ducks.

Homeless

Humans drain swamps to create land they can build on or cultivate. When this happens, wild ducks lose their shelter, breeding places, and sources of food—their habitats are destroyed. Also, many wetlands where ducks live are polluted by toxic wastes that are dumped into them by factories and large farms.

Once marshes are drained there is no more water to support a duck's life.

Lead poisoning

Ducks also get lead poisoning by accidentally swallowing hunters' cartridges that are left over from fired bullets. These cartridges remain in the mud, and ducks mistake them for food.

Hunters hide in "blinds," such as the wooden structure seen in the photo on the left. A blind is a hidden place from which hunters can shoot ducks.

On the farm

Unfortunately for ducks, they make for very tasty food. For centuries, people have domesticated them. Ducks are raised on farms in great numbers so people can gather their eggs or eat their meat. People also gather duck feathers and down to make pillows and feather beds.

Soft and warm, down is used in feather beds.

23

Cousins

Ducks are part of the Anatidae family, along with swans and geese. All of these waterfowl have round bodies, webbed feet, and a flat bill that is lined with plates. They fly and swim well, but on the ground, most of them waddle. There are dabbling ducks, such as the mallard, and diving ducks, such as the common pochard.

mute swan

Mute swans can be recognized by their red bill. Almost domesticated, mute swans live in lakes, usually in parks on the East Coast. Mute swans are usually quiet, but they make a whistling, hissing sound when angry.

Greylag geese are very noisy when they communicate, even when they are flying. Family life is important to them, and geese couples often mate for life. These European wild geese are vegetarian and migrate great distances.

greylag geese

24

common pochard

common teal

Common pochards are diving ducks, meaning their entire body can go underwater. Because their wings are smaller than those of dabbling ducks, pochards need a running start across the water to take off into the air. Common pochards can be found in Europe and Asia.

Common teals are small, wild ducks that are found throughout the Northern Hemisphere. They are the smallest of the dabbling ducks. Common teals dabble in shallow water and mud, looking for seeds.

muscovy ducks

Muscovy ducks are large domesticated ducks that do not fly. Wild muscovies do fly and can be found in both Central and South America. Most muscovies are black, but they can also be white or patched.

25

You'll find the answers to these questions in your book.

Index

Photograph credits:

Colibri Agency: P. Chefson: back cover, 12 (bottom left); A.–M. Loubsens: title page, 5 (top left), 6 (right inset), 10 (bottom), 10–11 (top), 20 (bottom), 24 (top), 25 (top left, bottom); A. Auricoste: 2 (inset); G. Abadie: 2–3; Negro/Cretu: 4; Cosnefroy: 5 (top right); Ch. Testu: 5 (bottom); Loubsens/Dequiedt: 6–7, 16 (bottom); R. Tonnel: 6 (left inset); C. Villette: 7 (inset); 12–13; M. Queral: 8–9; S. Bonneau: 8 (bottom); A. Roussel: 9 (bottom left), 21; C. Baranger: 9 (bottom right); B. Bonnal: 10 (top left), 25 (top right); J.–Y. Lavergne: 11 (bottom); G. Bonnafous: cover, 13 (top right); F. Merlet: 14; A. Labat: 15 (top); P. Ricard: 15 (bottom), 16 (top); M. Rhor: 17 (top); P. Neveu: 17 (bottom); A. Saunier: 18 (bottom left); Ph. Granval: 18–19, 22 (bottom); J.–M. Brunet: 19 (top right); J. Ginestous: 20 (top); A. Guerrier: 22–23; S. Breal: 23 (bottom); J.–L. Ermel: 24 (bottom)